Welcome to ENTRE NOUS, the first language tape to teach you French as the French speak it, including colloquialisms, idiomatic expressions, and even slang. There are 41 dialogs to take you from the train station to the hotel to the theater to the restaurant. The method of this unique program by Colette Crosnier is easy to follow and fun to do.

Relax, and just as though you were listening to your favorite melody, let the rhythm and words take you to France. As you listen, you will gradually tune your ear to imitate the voices you hear. For only a few minutes a day, you can increase your understanding and fluency. As you become confident in your ability to speak and understand the language, each French-speaking person you meet will help you learn more. In no time at all you'll be speaking like a true native.

Use the text to follow the tape. When you are traveling, the booklet can act as a guide to the situations you, as a traveler, may encounter. Bonne chance et bon voyage!

ENTRE NOUS I

Copyright© 1986 by Colette Crosnier
All rights reserved.
Printed in the United States of America.
No part of this publication may be reproduced, stored in a retrieval system, or transmitted in any form or by an means electronic, mechanical, photocopying, recording, or otherwise, without the prior written permission of the publisher.

ISBN: 0-88432-140-1 text and cassette
  1-57970-121-3 text and cd
  1-57970-537-5 text only

Published by Audio Forum
One Orchard Park Road, Madison, CT 06443 U.S.A.
www.audioforum.com

SOMMAIRE

1	DANS LA RUE (On the street)	1
2	DANS UN JARDIN PUBLIC, COMPTINES (In a public park. Children's counting rhymes)	1
3	DANS UN JARDIN PUBLIC (suite) (In a public park—Continued)	2
4	LA MARCHANDE DE GLACES (The ice cream vendor)	2
5	LE MARCHAND DE BALLONS (The balloon vendor)	3
6	DANS UN AUTOCAR (In a tour bus)	3
7	DIRECTIONS NO. 1 (avec l'agent) (Directions No. 1)	5
8	DIRECTIONS NO. 2 (avec la fleuriste) (Directions No. 2)	6
9	DIRECTIONS NO. 3—POMPIDOU (Directions No. 3)	6
10	SUR LA ROUTE DANS UN VILLAGE DE NORMANDIE (On a road in a village in Normandy)	7
11	SUR LE BATEAU-MOUCHE (On the Bateau-mouche, the excursion boat)	7
12	DANS LE METRO (In the subway)	8
13	A LA STATION-SERVICE (At the service station)	8
14	AGENDA (Agenda)	9
15	TOURISTES FATIGUES (Tired tourists)	9
16	A L'OFFICE DU TOURISME (At the tourist bureau)	10
17	A LA BANQUE (At the bank)	10
18	DANS LE TRAIN (On the train)	11
19	A L'HOTEL, LE CLIENT N'A PAS DE CHANCE (At the hotel, the unlucky guest)	12
20	A L'HOTEL, LE CLIENT A DE LA CHANCE (At the hotel, the lucky guest)	12
21	LE PETIT DEJEUNER A L'HOTEL (Breakfast in the hotel)	13
22	DEPART DE L'HOTEL (Departure from the hotel)	14
23	UNE ETAPE, AU COMPTOIR D'UN CAFE (A stopover at the counter in a cafe)	14
24	A LA TERRASSE D'UN CAFE (At a sidewalk cafe)	14
25	AU MAGASIN (At the department store)	15
26	DEUX CAMPEURS DEVANT UNE AGENCE IMMOBILIERE (Two campers in front of a real estate agency)	16
27	A LA PARFUMERIE (At the perfume shop)	16
28	L'HEURE DE L'APERITIF (The happy hour)	17
29	AU RESTAURANT, LE PRIX FIXE (At the restaurant, fixed price)	17
30	AU RESTAURANT, MENU A LA CARTE (At the restaurant, a la carte menu)	18
31	LA CLIENTE DIFFICILE (A difficult customer)	19
32	A LA PHARMACIE (At the pharmacy)	20
33	LE TELEPHONE ET LE MEDECIN (The telephone and the doctor)	21
34	DANS UN TAXI (In a taxi)	21
35	LOCATION DE VOITURES (Car rental)	22
36	A L'AEROPORT (At the airport)	22
37	AU ZOO (At the zoo)	23
38	A LA GARE (At the station)	23
39	A LA TOUR EIFFEL (At the Eiffel Tower)	24
40	UNE RENCONTRE (An encounter)	25
41	ARRIVEE A PARIS (Arrival in Paris)	26
	ENGLISH TRANSLATIONS OF MINI-DIALOGS	27

1. DANS LA RUE

— Bonjour, Colette.
— Bonjour, Michèle.
— Comment allez-vous?
— Très bien, merci, et vous?
— Je vais bien, merci.
— Comment va votre mari?
— Il va bien, et comment va votre fille?
— Pas mal, merci. Il fait beau, n'est-ce pas?
— Oui, il fait très beau. Je vais au marché acheter des légumes et à la boucherie acheter de la viande. Et où allez-vous?
— Je vais à la banque, à la poste, à la crèmerie, à la charcuterie, à la boulangerie . . . . Excusez-moi, je suis pressée.
— Moi aussi, je suis pressée, au revoir.
— Au revoir, à bientôt.

French people shop for fresh food every day. Though supermarkets *(supermarchés)* are becoming more popular, many homemakers still prefer open-air markets to insure the freshness of their vegetables and fruit. They also have their favorite butcher shop, bakery, delicatessen, cheese shop, etc. for their meat, bread, paté, cheese.

2. DANS UN JARDIN PUBLIC, COMPTINES

— Un, deux, trois,
  Allons dans les bois,
  Quatre, cinq, six,
  Cueillir des cerises,
  Sept, huit, neuf,
  Dans mon panier neuf,
  Dix, onze, douze,
  Elles seront toutes rouges.

— Quinze sur quinze,
  Revenez sur quinze,
  Quinze sur quinze,
  Quinze les voici!

The children are singing a popular counting rhyme while jumping rope.

3. JARDIN PUBLIC (SUITE)

– Bonjour!
– Bonjour Madame.
– Comment vous appelez-vous?
– Je m'appelle Jean-Pierre et ma sœur s'appelle Sophie.
– Et votre chien, comment s'appelle-t-il?
– Il s'appelle Jacky.
– Bonjour, Jacky.
– Oua, oua!
– Il est très beau.
– Oui, il est très beau et il est très intelligent.
– Quel âge a-t-il?
– Il a deux ans.
– Et vous deux, quel âge avez-vous?
– J'ai huit ans, ma petite sœur a quatre ans. Et vous Madame, quel âge avez-vous?
– Ah, ah, ah, mon âge est un secret!

Comment vous appelez-vous?	*Je m'appelle Jean-Pierre.*	*Quel âge avez-vous?*
What is your name?	My name is Jean-Pierre.	How old are you?
Lit: What do you call yourself?	Lit: I call myself Jean-Pierre.	Lit: What age do you have?

4. LA MARCHANDE DE GLACES

– Je voudrais deux cornets de glace, s'il vous plaît.
– Simples, ou doubles?
– Simples.
– Quels parfums avez-vous?
– J'ai vanille, chocolat, fraise, pistache et café.
– Un cornet de fraise pour moi et un cornet de chocolat pour Sophie.
– Voilà, petits, c'est 12 F.
– Et voilà 20 F.
– Vous n'avez pas de monnaie?
– De la monnaie? Non, j'ai deux pièces de 10 F, c'est tout.
– Bon d'accord, voilà 8 F de monnaie, une pièce de 5 F, et 3 pièces d'un Franc, 13, 14, 15, 16, 17, 18, 19, 20. Ca fait 20 F.
– Merci, Madame.
– Au revoir, les enfants!

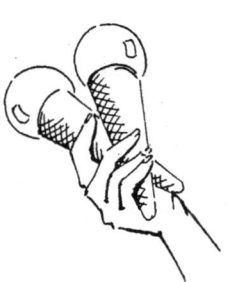

Notice the French word *monnaie*; it doesn't mean *money*, but "change". The word "money" is translated by *l'argent*.

5. LE MARCHAND DE BALLONS

- Les beaux ballons, qui veut un ballon, bleu, rouge, vert, jaune, orange, violet? Nous avons toutes les couleurs.
- Jean-Pierre, je veux un ballon.
- Quelle couleur?
- Un ballon rose.
- Bonjour, Monsieur, avez-vous un ballon rose?
- Je n'ai pas de ballon rose, mais voici un ballon rouge, ça va?
- Ça va, Sophie?
- Non, *Je veux* un ballon rose, je *ne veux pas* un ballon rouge.
- Et un ballon multicolore, c'est très joli.
- Oui, c'est joli.
- Alors voilà un ballon multicolore, ça fait 8 F.
- Violà 8 F et . . . je n'ai plus d'argent.
- Ballons, qui veut un ballon? Les beaux ballons, bleu, orange, rouge, vert, jaune, orange, violet, multicolore!! Ballons, ballons . . .

Je veux can be translated by "I want" or "I demand". It isn't considered polite to ask for something in this manner. One should say: *Je voudrais*. For example, *Je voudrais un ballon* is "I would like a balloon".

6. DANS UN AUTOCAR

- Vous êtes américaine?
- Non, je ne suis pas américaine, je suis canadienne.
- Et votre mari, est-ce qu'il est américain?
- Non, il est canadien aussi, nous sommes canadiens tous les deux. Et vous êtes française?
- Non, je ne suis pas française, je suis belge, je suis née à Bruxelles. Et vous Madame, où êtes-vous née?
- Je suis née à Montréal, mon mari est né à Québec.
- Est-ce que c'est votre premier voyage en France?
- Oui, c'est le premier.
- La France est belle, n'est-ce pas?
- Oui, très belle.
- Vous parlez bien français.
- C'est normal pour les canadiens français; et vous parlez bien français aussi.

- C'est normal pour les belges!
- Où habitez-vous au Canada?
- Nous habitons à Vancouver, dans l'Ouest. C'est une belle ville.
- Moi, j'habite à Liège. Ce n'est pas une belle ville. Je préfère Paris.
- Est-ce que vous venez souvent à Paris?
- Non, je ne viens pas souvent à Paris, c'est dommage. Est-ce que vous avez des enfants?
- Non, je n'ai pas d'enfant, nous n'avons pas d'enfant . . . c'est dommage, et vous?
- J'ai un fils et une fille, mais mon mari est mort, je suis veuve.
- Oh . . . je m'appelle Suzanne Guillaume.
- Enchantée, Madame, je m'appelle Madame Duchêne et je vous présente mon petit-fils Robert. Il voyage avec moi.
- Bonjour, Robert.
- Bonjour, Madame.
- Voilà, nous sommes arrivés, le tour commence, nous descendons—Vite, Robert, descendons.
  (Elle réveille le mari endormi.)
- Réveille-toi Pierre, nous sommes arrivés!
- Au revoir.
- Au revoir, à plus tard!
- Oui, à plus tard!

Autocar can be abbreviated by the word *car*. It is a coach used for tour groups or excursions. *L'autobus* is a bus for urban transportation only.

7. DIRECTIONS N°1

– Pardon, Monsieur l'agent, montrez-moi sur le plan où est l'Arc de Triomphe, s'il vous plaît.
– Voilà Mademoiselle, ici.
– Est-ce qu'il est sur la rive droite ou sur la rive gauche?
– Sur la rive droite et voici les Champs-Elysées, ici, la Place Vendôme là, le Louvre là-bas.
– Et où est l'église de la Madeleine?
– La Madeleine est entre la Place de la Concorde et l'Opéra.
– Ah oui, "l'O-pra"!
– Non Mademoiselle, l'O-PE-RA.
– C'est difficile, l'O-pé-ra".
– C'est ça, bravo.
– Et où est le musée du "Jus de Pomme"?
– Le "Jus de Pomme"?
– Oui, les Impressionnistes!
– Ah, le "Jeu de Paume"! Voilà, au coin de la rue de Rivoli et du Jardin des Tuileries, là, à gauche.
– Merci Monsieur.
– A votre service, Mademoiselle.

When you wish to speak to a stranger in the street to ask for directions, or if you wish to ask for information from anyone, start your sentence by: *Pardon, Monsieur; Pardon, Madame;* or *Pardon, Mademoiselle.* The French are formal with strangers. When you enter a store, you greet the salesperson with, *Bonjour, Monsieur (Madame, Mademoiselle)* and add these "titles" after *merci* (thank you) and *au revoir* (good-bye). Notice that the words "you are welcome" may be expressed in different ways by the French:

- *Je vous en prie* (more formal)
- *De rien* (casual)
- *A votre service* (by an employee to a customer)

L'Arc de Triomphe, la Place Vendôme, and la Madeleine are famous sights in Paris. Les Champs-Elysées is the most famous avenue, lined with cafés and luxurious shops. Le Musée du Jeu de Paume houses the national collection of Impressionist paintings. Watch for the pronunciation: *Jeu de Paume* could end sounding like *jus de pomme*, meaning "apple juice"!

8. DIRECTIONS N°2

- Pardon, Madame, quel autobus va à la Tour Eiffel?
- Prenez le numéro 69, c'est direct.
- Où est l'arrêt d'autobus?
- Devant le fleuriste, à côté du Prisunic, là derrière vous.
- Excusez-moi, je ne comprends pas; répétez plus lentement, s'il vous plaît.
- L'arrêt d'autobus est en face du fleuriste, à côté du Prisunic, là, le magasin Prisunic.
- Merci, Madame.
- Je vous en prie, Mademoiselle, bonne chance!

9. DIRECTIONS N°3

- Pardon Monsieur, nous sommes perdus, nous cherchons le Centre Beaubourg.
- Ah oui, le Centre Pompidou!
- Non, le Centre Beaubourg.
- Pompidou, Beaubourg, c'est la même chose. Il est tout droit devant vous, continuez tout droit.
- Ah oui, à droite!
- Attention, Monsieur, pas *à droite* mais *tout droit*, straight ahead.
- Ah, je comprends. C'est loin?
- Non Monsieur, ce n'est pas loin, c'est près, c'est à cinq minutes d'ici.
- Merci.
- De rien.

Le Centre Pompidou is also referred to as Centre Beaubourg. It is a multi-purpose cultural center built near the site of the former Halles market.

Tout droit means "straight ahead". *A droite* means "to the right". Watch for the pronunciation of the "t" in *droite*.

10. SUR LA ROUTE DANS UN VILLAGE DE NORMANDIE

- Pardon, Madame, je cherche Vernon, est-ce que c'est près d'ici?
- Vernon, Vernon, attendez, ah oui, vous êtes sur la mauvaise route, vous lui tournez le dos.
- Excusez-moi, je ne comprends pas, parlez plus lentement, s'il vous plaît.
- Bon, je répète "vous lui tournez le dos", mauvaise direction, vous comprenez?
- Ah oui, je comprends, montrez-moi sur la carte, s'il vous plaît.
- Voilà, vous êtes ici à Louviers, et Vernon est là dans l'autre direction.
- Ah oui, je vois, c'est à combien de kilomètres?
- 25 kms. Ce n'est pas loin si vous prenez l'autoroute.
- Et où est l'autoroute?
- Allez jusqu'à la place du marché, suivez les panneaux direction *est*.
- D'accord, merci.
- Vous parlez bien français.
- Oui, je parle un peu, mais je ne comprends pas bien.
- Patience, patience!

Vernon et Louviers are towns in Normandy, 50 km west of Paris, not far from Giverny (See dialog 13.)

Note the expression *vous lui tournez le dos* which is literally translated by "you are turning your back to it".

11. SUR LE BATEAU–MOUCHE

- Le Guide:
- Welcome aboard! Soyez les bienvenus à bord des Bateaux-Mouche!
- Et voici la Tour Eiffel à droite et le Palais de Chaillot.
- Nous passons sous le pont de l'Alma et à gauche, remarquez le Grand Palais, la Place de la Concorde et le Louvre.
- Nous passons sous le Pont-Neuf, le plus vieux pont de Paris et voici l'Ile de la Cité, le Palais de Justice et la Sainte Chapelle, la Cathédrale de Notre-Dame.
- N'oubliez pas de prendre une photo!
- Et maintenant nous retournons à la Tour Eiffel . . .
- La promenade est terminée.
- Merci Mesdames et Messieurs, et bon séjour à Paris et n'oubliez pas le guide!
- Merci!

The *bateaux-mouches* are excursion boats that offer a mini-cruise on the Seine, a wonderful way to see the major buildings along the left and right bank of the Seine.

12. DANS LE METRO

– Un carnet, s'il vous plaît; c'est combien?
– C'est 26 F.
– Voici 50 F.
– Vous avez de la monnaie?
– Oui, attendez, 10 F, encore 10 F et voilà 6 F.

Un peu plus tard:
– Pardon, quelle est la station pour Notre-Dame? Oui, pour Notre-Dame et la Sainte Chapelle?
– Ah oui, il faut descendre à Cité, mais ce n'est pas direct, regardez le plan.
– Oui, je vois.
– Vous êtes ici à Etoile-Charles de Gaulle. Prenez la direction Château de Vincennes; là, vous voyez; puis vous prenez la direction Porte d'Orléans et vous descendez à Cité.
– C'est difficile!
– Non, c'est facile, le métro parisien est très facile et il est rapide!

Métro is the abbreviation of "Métropolitian". It is a quick and efficient way to travel throughout Paris. You can buy a single ticket (*un ticket*) or a book of ten tickets (*un carnet*), which is more economical. Note that one ticket is good for unlimited rides provided that the rider remains underground.

13. A LA STATION SERVICE

– Le plein, s'il vous plaît.
– Super ou ordinaire?
– Super.
– Et l'huile, c'est bon?
– Oui c'est bon, merci. Avez-vous une carte de la région?
– Oui, bien sûr, où allez-vous?
– A Giverny, visiter le musée Claude Monet.
– Voilà, vous êtes ici sur l'autoroute de Normandie, allez tout droit, direction ouest, prenez la sortie Bonnières, continuez direction nord, vous passez le Grand Val, le Petit Val, prenez le pont, là, il traverse la Seine et tournez à droite, et vous êtes tout de suite arrivée à Giverny.
– Tout de suite, qu'est-ce que ça veut dire en kilomètres?
– 5 kms, peut-être. Je vous donne un dépliant, lisez: "Le musée est ouvert tous les jours de 10 H à 12 H et de 14 H à 18 H, du premier avril au 31 octobre. Fermeture le lundi."
– Merci, vous êtes bien aimable.
– A votre service, pour l'essence ça fait 200 F.
– Voilà.
– Merci, c'est juste. Bonne route!

Giverny is a small town in Normandy, 53 kilometers northwest of Paris. Claude Monet's country estate there has been a museum since 1980. Many of the artist's best-known paintings were inspired by its beautiful gardens.

Note that the French word for gasoline is *essence*, not *pétrole*.

14. AGENDA

- Quel est le programme cette semaine?
- Lundi, il y a beaucoup de magasins fermés, allons visiter la Tour Eiffel.
- Mardi, les musées sont fermés.
- Oui, mais les magasins sont ouverts, allons au Printemps et aux Galeries Lafayette.
- Et mercredi?
- Mercredi, les musées sont ouverts, allons au Louvre et au Jeu de Paume.
- Jeudi, allons visiter le Marais.
- Et vendredi?
- Vendredi, nous allons à Versailles et samedi nous visitons Montmartre et l'église du Sacré-Cœur.
- Dimanche?
- Dimanche, je suis fatigué, je reste à l'hôtel.
- Moi aussi, je me repose.
- Dimanche, restons à l'hôtel!

Many shops and even larger stores are closed for all or part of Monday. The Louvre and the Jeu de Paume are closed on Tuesday.

Le Marais (lit. the swamp) is a fashionable quarter that holds architectural treasures. Some of them have been restored after many years of neglect. Versailles, the palace of palaces! Surrounded by unforgettable gardens, a must for the foreign visitor. Montmartre, a part of Paris that is most picturesque, has retained the charm of an old-time village.

15. TOURISTES FATIGUES

- Le Guide: Comment ça va, les touristes?
- Je suis fatigué!
- Je ne suis pas fatiguée, j'ai faim!
- Je n'ai pas faim, j'ai soif!
- Je n'ai pas soif, j'ai chaud!
- Moi, je n'ai pas chaud, j'ai mal à la tête!
- J'ai mal à la tête et j'ai mal aux pieds!
- J'ai perdu ma carte!
- Où est mon appareil?
- Où sont mes lunettes de soleil?
- Avez-vous de l'aspirine?
- Non, je regrette, je n'ai pas d'aspirine.
- Je voudrais dormir!
- Je voudrais aller à l'hôtel!
- A quelle heure est le dîner?
- Le Guide: A 19 h. Courage, mes amis, encore deux églises et la visite d'un atelier de poterie et . . . c'est l'heure du dîner. En route!

Note that *j'ai faim*, literally translated "I have hunger," is translated in English "I am hungry." The same applies to *j'ai soif*, or "I am thirsty" in English; *j'ai chaud*, "I am hot"; and *j'ai froid*, "I am cold."

16. A L'OFFICE DE TOURISME

— Bonjour Mademoiselle, est-ce qu'il y a un bon hôtel près d'ici?
— Oui, l'hôtel Richelieu est très confortable.
— Est-ce qu'il est cher?
— Non, il est très raisonnable.
— Est-ce que vous recommandez un restaurant?
— Oui, "l'Alouette" est un excellent restaurant, bonne cuisine régionale—"Le Soleil d'Or" est aussi très bon, mais plus cher—"La Petite Auberge" est un deux étoiles, c'est un restaurant gastronomique.
— Non, ce n'est pas pour nous! Est-ce qu'il y a un musée dans la ville?
— Non, il n'y a pas de musée, mais il y a une belle cathédrale gothique.
— Est-ce qu'il y a un château?
— Oui, il y a un château et un beau parc avec une petite chapelle— C'est très intéressant, voici un dépliant et les heures de visite.
— Est-ce qu'il y a aussi une banque près d'ici? J'ai besoin de changer des chèques de voyage.
— Oui, il y a une banque au carrefour de la rue de la Gare et de la rue du Château. Mais dépêchez-vous, la banque ferme de midi à 14 H. . . . et il est 11 H et demi, dépêchez-vous!

L'office du tourisme is a wonderful place to gather free information. Every town has its own tourist office. The receptionist will inform the visitor about hotels, restaurants, and places of interest, and will offer a map of the town. Restaurants are rated by the number of stars.

In Paris, banks are open from 9.30 A.M. to 4.30 P.M. In smaller towns, they close during the lunch hour. French time is based on the 24-hour clock. 1 PM is equivalent to 13H00. 8 PM is 20H00.

17. A LA BANQUE

— Je voudrais changer des chèques de voyage, s'il vous plaît, ils sont en dollars.
— Bien, vous avez une pièce d'identité?
— Une pièce d'identité, je ne comprends pas.
— Un passeport.
— Oh, un passeport, voilà.
— Pour combien?
— Pour 200 dollars, quel est le cours aujourd'hui?
— Il est à 10,04 F. Signez ici s'il vous plaît. Voilà, ça fait 2.040 F, deux billets de 500 F, cinq billets de 100 F et quatre pièces de 10 F.
— Merci, c'est exact.
— Je vous en prie.

18. DANS LE TRAIN

— Pardon, cette place est occupée?
— Non, elle n'est pas occupée, elle est libre, asseyez-vous. Est-ce que je peux monter votre valise?
— Oui, merci.
— Vous désirez lire le journal?
— Non, merci.
— Où allez-vous Mademoiselle?
— Je vais à Bordeaux.
— Quelle coincidence, je vais à Bordeaux aussi.
— A quelle heure est-ce que le train arrive à Bordeaux?
— Il arrive à 18 H 30, et pourquoi est-ce que vous allez à Bordeaux?
— Je vais voir ma sœur, mon beau-frère et mes neveux, et vous?
— Je vais à Bordeaux, pour affaires.
— Ah oui, et dans quelles affaires êtes-vous?
— Affaires de vin, import-export . . . le vin de Bordeaux, et quelle est votre profession, Mademoiselle?
— Je suis secrétaire.
— Ma femme est secrétaire aussi, à Paris, quelle coincidence!
— Votre femme?
— Oui, ma femme, elle travaille à Paris, nous habitons à Paris, nous avons trois enfants. Vous désirez boire quelque chose au wagon-restaurant?
— Non merci, je n'ai pas soif et je n'ai pas faim. Excusez-moi, je suis fatiguée, j'ai sommeil et je vais dormir.

19. A L'HOTEL, LE CLIENT N'A PAS DE CHANCE

— Bonsoir Monsieur.
— Bonsoir Madame, est-ce que vous avez une chambre pour la nuit, deux personnes?
— Vous avez une réservation?
— Non, nous n'avons pas de réservation.
— Je regrette, monsieur, l'hôtel est complet.
— COMPLET!
— Oui, désolé, nous n'avons pas de place.
— Est-ce que vous recommandez un autre hôtel?
— Pas ce soir, tous les hôtels sont complets, un congrès, vous comprenez?
— C'est épouvantable, ma femme est malade, et nous sommes fatigués.
— Attendez, je vais téléphoner à Chinon. C'est à 60 kms, ça ne fait rien?
— Non, ça ne fait rien.
— Allô, bonsoir. Ici l'Hôtel des Châteaux, à Tours. Vous avez une chambre pour deux? Oui, oui, c'est une petite chambre, sans salle de bain, oui, oui, au troisième, oui. (Parlant au client): Une petite chambre sans salle de bain, au troisième? Ca va?
— Oui, ça va, merci.
— Oui, ça va, merci. (Au client): Quel nom?
— Gaveau.
— Au nom de Gaveau, au revoir!
— Merci, merci beaucoup. En route, Monique, nous avons une chambre.

Note the different meanings of the word *complet*. In this case, it means "full up". *L'autobus est complet*, "the bus is full up". Watch for another meaning in dialog 21.

The French number their floors starting at the first level above the street. The American first floor corresponds to *le rez-de-chaussée* (ground floor). Consequently, *le premier étage*, (first floor up) corresponds to the American second floor.

20. A L'HOTEL, LE CLIENT A DE LA CHANCE

— Bonsoir Madame.
— Bonsoir Monsieur.
— Nous avons une réservation.
— Oui, à quel nom?
— Dupré, René Dupré.
— Certainement, trois nuits, chambre avec salle de bain et W.C. Votre chambre est prête, montez avec moi, l'ascenseur est à gauche, je prends vos

valises. Voici la chambre N°29, après vous, entrez.
- Merci.
- Voici la salle de bain avec la douche, les serviettes, les oreillers dans la penderie et voici la clé.
- Mais il y a deux lits, nous préférons un lit.
- Ah oui, un grand lit.
- Une chambre à un lit, vous avez de la chance, la chambre 27 est libre et elle a un grand lit, suivez-moi s'il vous plaît.

- Voilà, c'est bien?
- C'est parfait, Madame, quel est le tarif?
- 400 F par nuit.
- Bien merci.
- A votre service et bon séjour! Pour le petit déjeuner, vous téléphonez demain matin.

21. LE PETIT DEJEUNER A L'HOTEL

- Allo, allo!
- Bonjour Mademoiselle.
- Bonjour Monsieur.
- Deux petits déjeuners chambre 27, s'il vous plaît.
- Café, thé, chocolat?
- Un café au lait et un thé.
- Bon, un café au lait et un thé complets.
- Complets, excusez-moi, je ne comprends pas, qu'est-ce que ça veut dire "complet"?
- Complet, ça veut dire qu'avec le café, vous avez aussi des croissants, du pain, du beurre, de la confiture.
- Et un œuf?
- Ah non, Monsieur, pas d'œuf.
- Et un jus d'orange?
- Un jus d'orange, avec un supplément.
- Est-ce que le petit déjeuner est compris dans le tarif de la chambre?
- Ah non, Monsieur, il n'est pas compris, c'est 20 F.
- Bon d'accord, alors un café au lait complet et un thé complet et deux jus d'orange, en supplément.
- Tout de suite, Monsieur.

Café au lait complet is the equivalent of a continental breakfast with black coffee and hot milk. Tea or hot chocolate may be ordered instead of coffee and either one will be served with croissants, crusty bread, butter and jam. Sometimes orange juice is served depending on the hotel. The French breakfast is light. Don't expect eggs and bacon to be featured.

22. DEPART DE L'HOTEL

– Je voudrais la note, s'il vous plaît.
– Quel nom?
– Dupré.
– Ah oui, chambre 27.
– Trois nuits à 400 F et trois petits déjeuners à 20 F pour deux personnes, ça fait 1.320 F.
– Oui, c'est juste, est-ce que vous prenez les cartes de crédit?
– Certainement, Monsieur, Visa, American Express, Mastercharge, Eurocard. Ce sont vos bagages?
– Oui, ils sont à nous.
– Bon, allez chercher la voiture dans le parking, je vous aide avec les valises, je serai devant la porte.
– Merci.
– Je vous en prie.

23. UNE ETAPE—AU COMPTOIR D'UN CAFE

– Un café-crème, s'il vous plaît, et où sont les toilettes?
– Au sous-sol au bout du couloir.
– Au sous-sol?
– Oui, en bas, l'escalier est à gauche.
– Merci!

24. A LA TERRASSE D'UN CAFE

– Monsieur, Monsieur!
– Le garçon: Oui, qu'est-ce que vous désirez boire?
– Une bière pour moi.
– Garçon: Une pression?
– Oui, une pression.
– Un coca.
– Un vin blanc.
– Un jus de pomme.
– Le garçon: Vous désirez la carte?
– J'ai faim, je voudrais un croque-monsieur.
– La même chose pour moi.
– Un sandwich jambon.
– Rien pour moi.
– Le garçon: Voilà, tout de suite.

It is no longer proper to address a waiter by *Garçon*, which means "boy". Use *Monsieur* whenever you need to address a waiter or to attract his attention.

Croque-monsieur: sandwich of ham and cheese grilled and served hot.

25. AU MAGASIN

— Bonjour Madame.
— Bonjour Mademoiselle.
— Vous désirez voir quelque chose?
— Oui, je cherche quelques cadeaux.
— Et qu'est-ce que vous cherchez comme cadeaux?
— Je ne sais pas exactement, je cherche un cadeau pour ma sœur.
— Pour votre sœur? Un joli foulard, peut-être, des gants?
— Oui, un foulard, c'est une bonne idée, et je cherche aussi un cadeau pour mon frère.
— Pour votre frère . . ., un porte-feuille?
— Oui, un porte-feuille, et pour ma mère?
— Pour votre mère, attendez . . . une eau de toilette, des mouchoirs, un parfum, une petite boîte en porcelaine de Limoges?
— Oui, une petite boîte en Limoges, c'est un joli souvenir.
— Maintenant, j'ai besoin d'un cadeau pour mon père.
— Ah, une cravate, un livre?
— Oui, une cravate, bonne idée.
— Et pour ma nièce?
— Quel âge a-t-elle?
— Elle a quinze ans.
— Un collier ou des boucles d'oreilles, un bracelet?
— Oui, un bracelet, et pour mon neveu?
— Quel âge a-t-il?
— Il a dix ans.
— Un jeu "Les chiffres et les lettres". Vous avez une grande famille!
— Oui, j'ai une grande famille et je n'ai pas beaucoup d'argent . . .
— Mais vous avez des cartes de crédit.
— Oui, Dieu merci!

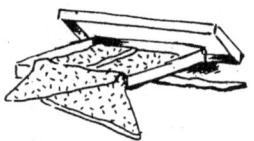

Porcelaine de Limoges: Limoges porcelain is renowned, and it is manufactured at Limoges, a city in central France.

Les chiffres et les lettres (numbers and letters) is a popular game for youngsters.

26. DEUX CAMPEURS DEVANT UNE AGENCE IMMOBILIÈRE

- Quelle belle maison!
- Oui, il y a une grande cuisine, un salon, une salle à manger, trois chambres, deux salles de bain.
- Un garage et un grand jardin avec terrasse et vue sur la mer, quel luxe!
- Est-ce que la location est chère?
- Je ne sais pas, il faut regarder l'affiche.
- Bon, je regarde: "A louer, au mois ou à la semaine, belle villa sur la Méditerranée, grande cuisine, salon, trois chambres, deux salles de bain, piscine .. ..". 3000 F la semaine.
- 3000 F!!!
- Oui, hélas, c'est trop cher pour notre budget, allons camper.
- Allons camper, en route, la vie est belle!

Note that the French word *location* doesn't express the same idea as in English. It means "rent" as in this dialogue or "rental" as in *location de bicyclettes* (bicycle rental).

27. A LA PARFUMERIE

- Bonjour Mademoiselle
- Bonjour Madame, qu'est-ce que vous désirez?
- Je voudrais acheter un parfum.
- Certainement, vous avez une préférence?
- Non, montrez-moi plusieurs marques, s'il vous plaît.
- Voilà, nous avons: Air du temps, Bal à Versailles, Ma griffe, Calèche, Chanel N°5, Chanel N°19, Madame Rochas, Vol de nuit, Amazone, tous les Diors . . . Diorissimo, Diorama . . .
- C'est tout?
- Non, nous avons aussi Vent vert, Gauloise, Eau de roche, Magie noire . . .
- Ah, quel choix difficile, qu'est-ce que vous recommandez?
- Opium, Madame, il sent très bon, il est à la mode, moi, j'adore Opium, vous désirez sentir?
- Oui, il sent très bon; c'est combien?
- 150 F le petit flacon pour le sac, 250 le grand flacon.
- Le choix est très difficile, je reviendrai.

La parfumerie doesn't only sell perfumes and eau de toilette but also cosmetics and fancy soaps.

28. L'HEURE DE L'APERITIF

- Qu'est-ce que vous désirez comme apéritif?
  C'est ma tournée.
- Un vermouth cassis.
- Je prendrai un Dubonnet avec un glaçon.
- Un Ricard pour moi.
- Un Martini.

Quelques minutes plus tard . . .

- Le garçon: Voilà un vermouth cassis pour Madame, un Dubonnet pour Mademoiselle, un Ricard pour Monsieur, et un Martini pour Monsieur.
- A votre santé!
- A la vôtre!
- Mais ce n'est pas un *Martini*, c'est du vermouth, c'est une erreur.
- Non, ce n'est pas une erreur, John, en France, un *Martini*, c'est du vermouth!

It is a tradition among the French people to sit in cafés to enjoy a refreshment or a light snack. During fair weather they sit outside at *la terrasse*, the part of the café set on the sidewalk. The French also love to gather with friends before the dinner hour for discussions and people-watching. They will sip an aperitif, a drink that incites the appetite (not to be confused with a cocktail, however).

Vermouth cassis is white Vermouth wine with a dash of black currant liqueur. Ricard is a popular anise flavored alcoholic drink which water is added to. Martini is a brand name of white vermouth wine.

29. AU RESTAURANT—LE PRIX FIXE

- Bonsoir.
- Bonsoir, une table pour deux?
- Oui, près de la fenêtre, s'il vous plaît.
- Ici?
- Oui, c'est très bien.
- Vous désirez un apéritif?
- Non merci, pas d'apéritif, la carte s'il vous plaît.
- Voici la carte, vous avez deux menus touristiques, un à 100 F et un à 150 F et vous avez aussi le menu gastronomique à 200 F. Il y a aussi le menu à la carte, je vous laisse faire votre choix.
- Mummm, le menu touristique est avantageux.
- Pourquoi?
- Parce qu'il y a le hors d'œuvre, l'entrée, le plat garni, le fromage, le dessert et le vin est compris.
- Oui, c'est avantageux.
- Quel est votre choix?
- Le menu touristique à 150 F.

- Et pour moi le menu gastronomique.
- Quel appétit vous avez!
- C'est vrai, mais la cuisine française est si bonne!

The word for lunch is *déjeuner*. The word for dinner is *dîner*.

French restaurants offer set menus which are more economical than ordering à la carte. They include an *hors d'oeuvre*, an appetizer; *l'entrée*, a first dish (not to be confused with the American entrée, which is the main dish). Then comes the main dish that is sometimes followed by a green salad. Cheese or dessert ends the meal.

30. AU RESTAURANT—MENU A LA CARTE

- Garçon: Bonsoir.
- Bonsoir Monsieur, une table pour trois, s'il vous plaît.
- A l'intérieur ou à la terrasse?
- A l'intérieur, il fait froid ce soir.
- Certainement, par ici, c'est bien?
- Oui, c'est très bien.
- Voici la carte, vous prendrez un apéritif?
- Bon, je voudrais un Cinzano.
- Oui, je prendrai un Ambassadeur.
- Je désire un St Raphaël.

- Quel choix! Qu'est-ce que vous recommandez?
- Comme hors-d'œuvre, le pâté de lapin ou les asperges vinaigrette.
- Et comme entrée?
- Le saumon en feuilleté ou la brochette de fruits de mer.
- Bon, un pâté de lapin et le saumon.
- Pour moi aussi.
- Je préfère les asperges vinaigrette et la brochette de fruits de mer.
- Et comme plat?
- Je prendrai le ris de veau, il est garni?
- Oui, tous les plats sont garnis de petits légumes.
- Pas pour moi, je préfère les côtes d'agneau grillées aux herbes de Provence.
- Et moi, une entrecôte marchand de vin.
- Comment désirez-vous l'entrecôte? Saignante, à point, bien cuite?
- A point.
- Bon, un ris de veau, une côte d'agneau et une entrecôte, vous voulez une salade?
- Non, pas de salade.
- Non merci.
- Oui, une salade.
- Vous prendrez un fromage ou un dessert?
- Un fromage, pas de dessert.
- Un dessert, s'il vous plaît.

- Un fromage *et* un dessert.
- Nous avons une coupe à l'ananas, un flan maison ou le délice aux framboises.
- La coupe à l'ananas.
- Le délice aux framboises.
- Et quel vin avec ça?
- Une bouteille de blanc, un Muscadet, et une bouteille de rouge, un Côte du Rhône.
- Deux bouteilles, c'est beaucoup, un petit pichet de blanc, peut-être, le vin de la maison?
- Bonne idée.
- Vous désirez aussi de l'eau minérale? Plate ou gazeuse?
- Oui, une grande bouteille, d'eau plate.
- Ce sera tout?
- Oui, ce sera tout.

Un peu plus tard . . .

- Quel bon dîner!
- Oui, quel bon dîner!
- Vous désirez un café?
- Oui, un café pour moi.
- Un café.
- Un déca, s'il vous plaît et l'addition.

Ambassadeur and St Raphaël are two popular brands of aperitifs. Wine accompanies the meal but so does mineral water. It has to be ordered separately: *eau plate:* plain water, *eau gazeuse:* carbonated water.

Coffee is served after dessert, never with the meal.

31. LA CLIENTE DIFFICILE

- Madame, vous désirez un apéritif?
- Non merci, pas d'apéritif.
- Vous désirez un hors d'œuvre?
- Non, pas de hors d'œuvre, je n'ai pas très faim. Quelle est la spécialité?
- Les fruits de mer, Madame.
- Je ne supporte pas les fruits de mer.
- Un steak, alors?
- Non, je ne mange pas de viande, qu'est-ce que vous avez comme légumes?
- Chou-fleur au gratin ou petits pois.
- Non, merci, je n'aime pas le chou-fleur, ni les petits pois.
- Une salade?

- Non, pas de salade.
- Un fromage, alors?
- Non, pas de fromage.
- Est-ce que vous désirez un dessert? Glace, pâtisserie, tarte, flan?
- Non, merci, je suis au régime.
- Désirez-vous du vin?
- Non, je ne bois pas de vin.
- De l'eau?
- Oui, j'ai soif, je voudrais une demi bouteille d'eau minérale . . . et l'addition.
- C'est *TOUT?*
- Oui, c'est tout. Un instant, fermez la fenêtre, s'il vous plaît, j'ai froid.
- Certainement Madame.

32. A LA PHARMACIE

- Bonjour Madame.
- Bonjour Madame.
- Je voudrais de l'aspirine.
- C'est pour vous?
- Oui, c'est pour moi.
- Une grande boîte ou une petite boîte?
- Une grande boîte mais . . . je ne suis pas malade.
- Et avec ça?
- Quelque chose pour la gorge.
- Mmm . . . Vous avez mal à la tête et à la gorge.
- Oui, mais . . . je ne suis pas malade.
- Est-ce que vous toussez?
- Oui, je tousse aussi, mais . . . je ne suis pas malade.
- Mmm . . . c'est peut-être un rhume. Vous avez de la température?
- Je ne sais pas, j'ai chaud.
- Mmm . . . Vous avez mal au ventre?
- Oui, j'ai un peu mal au ventre.
- Vous avez mal au cœur?
- Mal au cœur, *dans* le cœur?
- Non, mal au cœur, ça veut dire la nausée, c'est peut-être la grippe.
- Ah, mon Dieu, je suis malade, qu'est-ce que vous recommandez?
- De l'aspirine pour le mal de tête, des pastilles pour le mal de gorge et pour la toux et voici un médicament pour le ventre et restez au lit. Ca fait 80 F. Du repos, Madame, du repos, restez au lit et buvez du jus de fruit.
- Je suis étrangère, je voudrais le nom d'un médecin, vous avez une recommandation?
- Ah oui, le Docteur Vaudequin est excellent.

- Vous avez son numéro?
- Le 258-63-72.
- Ecrivez le numéro, s'il vous plaît.
- Voilà, Madame, j'écris le numéro et . . . du repos, du repos!!

A French pharmacy is not a drugstore. It only sells medicine, some medicated cosmetics, and a few medically related articles. The pharmacist is professionally trained and customers seek advice in case of minor illness.
Note that *mal au coeur* is translated literally by "sick to the heart" and it actually means "nauseous."

33. LE TELEPHONE ET LE MEDECIN

- Je vais téléphoner au Dr. Vaudequin. Je compose son numéro 258-63-72. 2-5-8-6-3- 7-2.
- Allô!
- Allô, Mademoiselle, je voudrais parler au Dr. Vaudequin, s'il vous plaît.
- C'est de la part de qui?
- Madame Duchêne.
- Vous êtes une malade du docteur?
- Non, je suis étrangère et je suis de passage.
- Un instant, ne quittez pas.
- Allô, c'est le Dr. Vaudequin à l'appareil, quels sont vos symptômes, Madame?
- Ah, bonjour docteur, je suis Madame Duchêne, j'ai mal à la tête, j'ai mal au cœur, j'ai mal à la gorge et je tousse.
- Mmm . . . Avez-vous de la température?
- Je ne sais pas, mais j'ai chaud.
- Prenez deux aspirines, buvez beaucoup de jus de fruit, restez au lit et téléphonez-moi demain matin si vous avez les mêmes symptômes. Du repos, Madame, du repos. Au revoir, Madame.

34. DANS UN TAXI

- Taxi!
- Oui Madame, où voulez-vous aller?
- A Montparnasse s'il vous plaît, au restaurant La Coupole. Est-ce que c'est loin?
- Non, c'est à vingt minutes, mais il y a beaucoup de circulation.
- Zut, mes amis m'attendent à midi et il est déjà 11h30! Faites vite, s'il vous plaît.
- Ah les clients, c'est toujours la même histoire "Faites vite, dépêchez-vous". Mais quelle vie!

Plus tard . . .

– Nous avons de la chance, il est midi et vous n'êtes pas en retard, vous êtes en avance de trois minutes.
– Merci, merci, c'est combien?
– Quarante francs, s'il vous plaît.
– Voici quarante francs et voici cinq francs pour vous.

La Coupole is an old and well-established restaurant in the district of Montparnasse in Paris. Famous French personalities can often be seen here. A 10% tip to the taxi driver is customary.

35. LOCATION DE VOITURE

– Est-ce que vous louez des voitures?
– Oui, bien sûr, qu'est-ce que vous recherchez?
– Une petite voiture. Quels sont vos tarifs?
– Nous avons le tarif week-end du vendredi soir au lundi matin. Ensuite nous avons un tarif spécial pour huit jours et pour quinze jours ou pour un mois. Pour combien de jours voulez-vous la voiture?
– Une semaine.
– Voulez-vous une assurance?
– Bien sûr.
– Le prix est de 500 francs la semaine pour une petite voiture avec assurance, Renault, Fiat, Peugeot, Toyota?
– Une Renault.
– Préparez votre passeport et votre permis de conduire, je suis à vous tout de suite.
– Merci.

36. A L'AEROPORT

– Pardon Monsieur. Nous cherchons un taxi pour aller à Paris.
– Sortez par la porte numéro 30, les taxis passent souvent.
– Combien coûte le taxi pour Paris?
– Environ 100 francs.
– C'est cher! Nous sommes des étudiants! Est-ce qu'il y a un train pour Paris?
– Oui, prenez l'autobus pour aller à la gare, l'arrêt est devant la porte numéro 25. Il y a un autobus toutes les 15 minutes pour la Gare du Nord à Paris.
– Combien coûte un billet de train?
– 25 francs.
– C'est parfait pour nous. Merci, prenons le train!

La Gare du Nord is a train station in Paris for departures to Northern France.

37. AU ZOO

– J'ai envie d'aller au zoo!
– Attendez, je regarde sur le guide. Oui, le Zoo de Vincennes est très réputé.
– Où est-il?
– Il est à Vincennes, là, au sud-est de Paris.
– Je vois, et comment y aller?
– Les directions sont très claires. Nous sommes ici, à l'Etoile, nous prenons le métro direction Vincennes jusqu'à Saint-Mandé-Tourelles, c'est direct. Là nous descendons et nous prenons l'autobus N°86 au coin de l'avenue Charles de Gaulle et de l'avenue de Paris. Le terminus est devant le zoo.

AU ZOO (suite)

Un peu plus tard . . .

– C'est un très beau zoo, j'aime regarder les animaux, les tigres, les lions, les panthères, les éléphants, les girafes.
– Je préfère les singes, ils sont si drôles!
– Et les oiseaux, ils sont magnifiques et il y a beaucoup d'espèces différentes.
– Je lis dans le guide "Michelin" qu'il y a 600 mammifères et 700 oiseaux dans ce parc qui est le plus riche de France.
– Oui, et je remarque avec joie que le cadre est naturel.
– Quelle liberté pour les animaux!

38. A LA GARE

– Je voudrais réserver un billet de T.G.V. pour Lyon.
– Pour quelle date?
– Le 5 septembre.
– Un aller simple ou un aller-retour?
– Un aller-retour.
– Première classe ou deuxième classe?
– Deuxième classe.
– Fumeur ou non fumeur?
– Non fumeur. Quelles sont les heures de départ?
– Il y a un départ toutes les demi-heures.
– Et combien de temps faut-il pour aller à Lyon?
– Il faut deux heures.

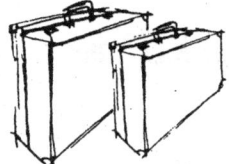

— C'est rapide!
— Oui, T.G.V. veut dire "train à grande vitesse".
— Bon, alors un aller-retour Lyon, deuxième classe, non fumeur, le 5 septembre, à 10h15.
— Voilà ça fait 600 francs.
— J'ai encore une question, est-ce qu'il y a un wagon-restaurant dans le train de 10h15?
— Non, mais il y a un mini-bar. N'oubliez pas de composter votre billet.
— Composter mon billet, je ne comprends pas, qu'est-ce que cela veut dire?
— Composter, c'est mettre votre billet dans le composteur, l'appareil orange prés du quai, pour marquer la date. Sinon votre billet n'est pas valable et vous risquez l'amende.
— Merci bien.
— De rien.

T.G.V. are the initials of *Train à grande vitesse*, which means "train at great speed". Reservations are required. All train tickets must be validated by an automatic machine, *le composteur*, before boarding.

39. A LA TOUR EIFFEL

— Est-ce que nous montons dans la Tour Eiffel?
— Bien sûr, nous sommes à Paris pour visiter tous les monuments.
— Nous avons le choix entre le premier étage, le deuxième étage ou le troisième étage; qu'est-ce que vous préférez?
— Allons au troisième, la vue sera sensationnelle.
— D'accord. Voici la queue pour prendre les billets.

Au guichet . . .
- Deux billets pour le troisième étage, s'il vous plait.
- Le troisième est fermé aujourd'hui.
- Ah, zut! Pourquoi est-ce que le troisième est fermé?
- Trop de monde, monsieur.
- Alors deux billets pour le deuxième.
- 44 francs, mettez-vous à la queue, l'ascenseur est au fond, à droite.
- Quelle foule!
- Ecoutez, on parle toutes les langues, ce n'est pas la Tour Eiffel, c'est la Tour de Babel!
- Vous avez votre plan pour identifier Paris?
- Oui, le voilà.

Sur la Tour . . .

- Quelle vue! Paris est gigantesque!
- Combien est-ce qu'il y a d'habitants?
- Deux millions.
- Regardez, la Seine, le Palais de Chaillot et tous les ponts.
- Et les bateaux-mouches sur la Seine.
- Je vois le Sacré-Cœur, là-bas, sur la colline.
- Regardez, les voitures sont toutes petites.
- Quel spectacle!
- Là, l'espace vert, c'est le Bois de Boulogne et là, c'est la Défense, le nouveau Paris, le petit Manhattan avec des gratte-ciel.
- Descendons au premier étage, il y a un restaurant, nous pouvons manger ou boire quelque chose.
- Bonne idée, est-ce que vous savez combien il y a de marches dans les escaliers de la Tour Eiffel?
- Oui, il y a 1652 marches.
- Oh, là, là!

The famous Eiffel Tower has three platforms. The third one is often closed, as it holds only a limited number of sightseers and in the summer crowds are very large. The first platform has an attractive restaurant and a tearoom. The second platform has a snackbar.

40. UNE RENCONTRE

- Colette!
- Michèle, quelle surprise!
- Et quelle journée!
- Qu'est-ce que vous avez fait?
- Je suis allée dans les grands magasins.

– Moi aussi, et dans quels magasins êtes-vous allée?
– Au Printemps et aux Galeries Lafayette.
– Je suis allée à la Samaritaine.
– Qu'est-ce que vous avez acheté?
– J'ai acheté beaucoup de choses: une robe, une jupe, deux blouses et des chaussures. Et vous?
– J'ai acheté un sac, des collants, une chemise de nuit et deux disques.

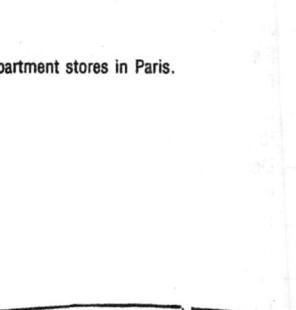

– Il y a beaucoup de soldes en ce moment, les prix sont formidables, mais quelle foule!
– Vous avez visité l'exposition d'antiquités au Printemps?
– Non, je n'ai pas visité l'exposition, mais j'ai vu des meubles, des tableaux et des tapis au rayon ameublement.
– Je suis allée au sous-sol et j'ai regardé la vaisselle, les casseroles et les verres.
– Pour vous?
– Non, je cherche un cadeau de mariage.
– Allons au salon de thé prendre une tasse de thé.
– Avec plaisir!

This dialogue gives a hint of one of the French past tenses.

Le Printemps, les Galeries Lafayette, and la Samaritaine are large department stores in Paris.

41. ARRIVEE A PARIS

– Mesdames, et Messieurs, nous aterrissons dans quelques minutes à l'aéroport Charles de Gaulle, regagnez vos sièges et attachez vos ceintures, éteignez vos cigarettes. Merci. Il est 14h30 heure locale et la température est de 20 degrés centigrades. Le Commandant Denis et son équipage vous remercient et vous souhaitent un excellent séjour en France.

– Cette hôtesse est vraiment charmante.
– Oh oui, regardez! L'autoroute, les maisons, les champs, les jardins, les voitures!
– Et les bateaux là-bas sur la rivière!
– Voilà, nous aterrissons.
– N'oubliez pas votre journal.
– Oh maintenant, je vais lire des journaux français.
– Vous parlez bien français.
– J'apprends avec une nouvelle méthode, "Entre nous", vous connaissez?
– Non, mais je compte sur vous.

ENGLISH TRANSLATIONS OF MINI-DIALOGS

CONTENTS

1	ON THE STREET	31
2	IN A PUBLIC PARK. CHILDREN'S COUNTING RHYMES	31
3	IN A PUBLIC PARK. (CONTINUED)	31
4	THE ICE CREAM VENDOR	32
5	THE BALLOON VENDOR	32
6	IN A TOUR BUS	32
7	DIRECTIONS NO. 1	33
8	DIRECTIONS NO. 2	34
9	DIRECTIONS NO. 3	34
10	ON A ROAD IN A VILLAGE IN NORMANDY	34
11	ON THE BATEAU-MOUCHE, THE EXCURSION BOAT	35
12	IN THE SUBWAY	35
13	AT THE SERVICE STATION	35
14	AGENDA	36
15	TIRED TOURISTS	36
16	AT THE TOURIST BUREAU	37
17	AT THE BANK	37
18	ON THE TRAIN	38
19	AT THE HOTEL, THE UNLUCKY GUEST	38
20	AT THE HOTEL, THE LUCKY GUEST	39
21	BREAKFAST IN THE HOTEL	39
22	DEPARTURE FROM THE HOTEL	40
23	A STOPOVER AT THE COUNTER IN A CAFE	40
24	AT A SIDEWALK CAFE	40
25	AT THE DEPARTMENT STORE	40
26	TWO CAMPERS IN FRONT OF A REAL ESTATE AGENCY	41
27	AT THE PERFUME SHOP	41
28	THE HAPPY HOUR	42
29	AT THE RESTUARANT, FIXED PRICE	42
30	AT THE RESTAURANT, A LA CARTE MENU	43
31	A DIFFICULT CUSTOMER	44
32	AT THE PHARMACY	44
33	THE TELEPHONE AND THE DOCTOR	45
34	IN A TAXI	46
35	CAR RENTAL	46
36	AT THE AIRPORT	46
37	AT THE ZOO	47
38	AT THE STATION	47
39	AT THE EIFFEL TOWER	48
40	AN ENCOUNTER	49
41	ARRIVAL IN PARIS	49

1. ON THE STREET

- Good day, Colette.
- Good day, Michele.
- How are you?
- Very well, and you?
- I am well too, thank you.
- How is your husband?
- He is well, and how is your daughter?
- Not bad, thank you. The weather is beautiful, isn't it?
- Yes, the weather is beautiful. I am going to the market to buy some vegetables and to the butcher shop to buy some meat. And where are you going?
- I am going to the bank, to the post office, to the dairy, to the delicatessen, to the bakery . . . Excuse me, I am in a hurry.
- Me too, I am in a hurry, goodbye.
- Goodbye, see you soon.

2. IN A PUBLIC PARK, CHILDREN'S COUNTING RHYMES

One, two, three,
Let's go to the woods,

Four, five, six,
to pick some cherries,

Seven, eight, nine,
in my new basket,

Ten, eleven, twelve,
they will be all red.

Fifteen on top of fifteen,
return to fifteen,

Fifteen on top of fifteen,
Fifteen, here they are!

3. IN A PUBLIC PARK

- Hello.
- Hello, Madame.
- What is your name?
- My name is Jean-Pierre, and my sister's name is Sophie.
- And your dog, what's his name?
- His name is Jacky.
- Hello, Jacky.
- Bow wow!
- He is very handsome.
- Yes, he is very handsome and he is very intelligent.
- How old is he?
- He is two years old.
- And you two, how old are you?
- I am eight and my little sister is four. And you Madame, how old are you?
- Ha, ha, ha, my age is a secret!

4. THE ICE CREAM VENDOR

- I would like two ice-cream cones, please.
- Single or double?
- Single, what flavors do you have?
- I have vanilla, chocolate, strawberry, pistachio, and coffee.
- A strawberry cone for me and a chocolate cone for Sophie.
- Here they are, kids, it's 12 francs.
- And here are 20 francs.
- You don't have any change?
- Some change? No, I have two 10 franc coins, that's all.
- All right, here are 8 francs in change: one 5 franc coin and three 1 franc coins, 13, 14, 15, 16, 17, 18, 19, 20—That's 20 francs.
- Thank you, Madame.
- Goodbye, children!

5. THE BALLOON VENDOR

- Beautiful balloons, who wants a balloon? Blue, red, green, yellow, orange, purple? We have every color.
- Jean-Pierre, I want a balloon.
- Not, "I want," Sophie, but "I would like."
- I would like a balloon.
- What color?
- A pink balloon.
- Hello, Sir, do you have a pink balloon?
- I don't have a pink balloon, but here is a red balloon, O.K.?
- O.K., Sophie?
- No, *I want* a pink balloon, I *don't want* a red balloon.
- And a multicolor balloon? It's very pretty.
- Yes, it's pretty.
- Then, here is a multicolor balloon, that's 8 francs.
- Here's 8 francs and . . . I don't have any more money.
- Balloons, who wants a balloon? Beautiful balloons, blue, orange, red, green, yellow, purple, multicolor!!! Balloons, Balloons!!

6. IN A TOUR BUS

- Are you American?
- No, I am not American, I am Canadian.
- And your husband, is he American?
- No, he is Canadian also. We are both Canadians. Are you French?
- No, I am not French, I am Belgian. I was born in Brussels. And you, Madame, where were you born?
- I was born in Montreal. My husband was born in Quebec.
- Is this your first trip to France?

- Yes, it is the first one.
- France is beautiful, isn't it?
- Yes, very beautiful.
- You speak French well.
- It's normal for French Canadians. And you speak French well too.
- It's normal for Belgians! Where do you live in Canada?
- We live in Vancouver, in the West. It's a beautiful city.
- As for me, I live in Liège, it's not a beautiful city. I prefer Paris.
- Do you come to Paris often?
- No, I don't come to Paris often, it's too bad—Do you have any children?
- No, I don't have any children . . . we don't have any children . . . it's too bad. And you?
- I have a son and a daughter, but my husband is dead. I am a widow.
- Oh . . . My name is Suzanne Guillaume.
- How do you do? My name is Madame Duchene and this is my grandson, Robert. He is travelling with me.
- Good day, Robert.
- Good day, Madame.
- Here we are, we have arrived, the tour is beginning, we get off. Quick, Robert, let's get off.
- Wake up, Pierre (She wakes the sleeping husband). We have arrived!
- Goodbye.
- Goodbye, see you later.
- Yes, until later.

7. DIRECTIONS N°1

- Pardon me, Mr. Policeman, show me on the map where the Arch of Triumph is, please.
- There it is Miss, here.
- Is it on the Right Bank or on the Left Bank?
- On the Right Bank, and here is the Champs-Elysées here, Vendôme Square there, the Louvre over there.
- And where is the Madeleine Church?
- The Madeleine is between the Concorde Square and the Opéra.
- Ah yes, "l'Op-ra."
- No, Miss, "L'O-pé-ra."
- It's difficult, "L'O-pé-ra."
- That's it, bravo!
- And where is the Museum of the "Jus de Pomme"?
- The "Apple Juice"?
- Yes, the Impressionists!
- Ah, the "Jeu de Paume"! There, on the corner on the street of Rivoli and the Garden of the Tuileries, there on the left.
- Thank you, Sir.
- At your service, Miss.

8. DIRECTIONS N°2

- Pardon me, Madame, what bus goes to the Eiffel Tower?
- Take number 69, it's direct.
- Where is the bus stop?
- In front of the florist, next to the Prisunic there, behind you.
- Excuse me, I don't understand, repeat more slowly, please.
- The bus stop is in front of the florist, next to the Prisunic; there, the Prisunic store.
- Thank you, Madame.
- You are welcome, Miss. Good luck!

9. DIRECTIONS N°3

- Pardon me, sir we are lost, we are looking for the Beaubourg Center.
- Yes, the Pompidou Center!
- No, the Beaubourg Center.
- Pompidou, Beaubourg, it's the same thing. It is straight ahead in front of you, continue straight ahead.
- Ah yes, to the right!
- Pay attention, sir, not *on the right* but, *straight ahead* (in English).
- Ah, I understand. Is it far?
- No Sir. It's not far, it's nearby. It's five minutes from here.
- Thank you.
- You are welcome.

10. ON A ROAD IN A VILLAGE IN NORMANDY

- Pardon me, Madame, I am looking for Vernon. Is it nearby?
- Vernon, Vernon . . . wait, ah yes, you are on the wrong road. Vernon is behind you.
- Excuse me, I don't understand. Speak more slowly, please.
- All right, I repeat: "Vernon is behind you, wrong direction." Do you understand?
- Ah yes, I understand. Show me on the map, please.
- So, you are here at Louviers, and Vernon is there in the other direction.
- Yes, I see, how many kilometers?
- 25 kilometers. It's not far if you take the freeway.
- And where is the freeway?
- Go to the market square, follow the signs direction East.
- O.K., thank you.
- You speak French well.
- Yes, I speak a little, but I don't understand very well.
- Patience, patience!

11. ON THE BATEAU-MOUCHE
(The excursion boat)

— The Guide:
— Welcome aboard! Welcome aboard the Bateaux-Mouches! And here's the Eiffel Tower on the right and the Palace of Chaillot. We are passing under the bridge of Alma and on the left, notice the "Grand Palais," the "Concorde Square," and the "Louvre".
— We are passing under the "Pont-Neuf," the oldest bridge in Paris, and here's the island of "la Cité" with the Palace of Justice, the "Sainte-Chapelle" and the Cathedral of Notre Dame.
— Don't forget to take a picture. And now we are returning to the Eiffel Tower . . .
— The excursion is over.
— Thank you, ladies and gentlemen. Have a good stay in Paris and don't forget the guide!
— Thank you.

12. IN THE SUBWAY

— A book of tickets, please. How much is it?
— It's 26 francs.
— Here are 50 francs.
— Do you have any change?
— Yes, wait, 10 francs, another 10 francs and here are 6 francs.

A little later . . .

— Pardon me, what is the stop for Notre-Dame? Yes, for Notre-Dame and the Sainte-Chapelle?
— Ah yes, you must get off at "Cité," but it's not direct. Look on the map.
— Yes, I see.
— You are here at "Etoile-Charles de Gaulle," take the direction "Château de Vincennes"; there, you see? Then you take the direction "Porte d'Orléans" and you get of at "Cité".
— It's difficult.
— No, it's easy. The Parisian subway is very easy and it is fast!

13. AT THE SERVICE STATION

— Fill it up, please.
— Super or regular?
— Super.
— And the oil, it's all right?
— Yes, it's all right, thank you. Do you have a map of the region?

- Yes, of course, where are you going?
- To Giverny to visit the Claude Monet Museum.
- You are here, on the Normandy Freeway, go straight ahead, direction West, take the Bonnières exit, continue North. You pass the Grand Val, Le Petit Val; take the bridge, there, it crosses the Seine; turn to the right and right away you have arrived at Giverny.
- Right away, what does it mean in kilometers?
- Five kilometers, maybe. I am giving you a brochure. Read: "The museum is open every day from 10 A.M. to 12 and from 14H to 18H from the first of April to October 31st. Closed on Monday."
- Thank you, you are very kind.
- At your service. For the gas, it's 200 francs.
- There it is.
- Thank you, it's just right. Have a good trip!

14. AGENDA

- What's the program for this week?
- On Monday, there are many stores that are closed. Let's go visit the Eiffel Tower.
- On Tuesday, the museums are closed.
- Yes, but the stores are open; let's go to the "Printemps" and to the "Galeries Lafayette."
- And on Wednesday?
- On Wednesday, the museums are open; let's go to the Louvre and to the "Jeu de Paume."
- On Thursday, let's go and visit the Marais.
- And on Friday?
- On Friday, we go to Versailles, and on Saturday, we visit Montmartre and the Church of the Sacred Heart.
- On Sunday?
- On Sunday, I am tired; I'll stay in the hotel.
- Me too, I rest. On Sunday, let's stay in the hotel!

15. TIRED TOURISTS

- The guide: How is it going, tourists?
- I am tired!
- I am not tired, I am hungry!
- I am not hungry, I am thirsty!
- I am not thirsty, I am hot!
- As for me, I am not hot, I have a headache!
- I have a headache and my feet ache!
- I have lost my map.
- Where is my camera?

- Where are my sunglasses?
- Do you have any aspirin?
- No, I am sorry, I don't have any aspirin.
- I would like to go to sleep!
- I would like to go to the hotel.
- At what time is dinner?
- The guide: At 7 PM. Courage, my friends. Two more churches and a visit to a pottery studio and . . . it's time for dinner—Let's hit the road!

16. AT THE TOURIST BUREAU

- Good day, Miss, is there a good hotel nearby?
- Yes, the Hotel Richelieu is very comfortable.
- Is it expensive?
- No, it's very reasonable.
- Can you recommend a restaurant?
- Yes, "L'Alouette" (the Lark) is an excellent restaurant, good local food. "Le Soleil d'Or" (the Golden Sun) is also very good, but more expensive. "La Petite Auberge" (the Little Inn) is a "two stars," it is a gourmet restaurant.
- No, it is not for us! Is there a museum in the town?
- No, there is no museum, but there is a beautiful Gothic cathedral.
- Is there a castle?
- Yes, there is a castle and a beautiful park with a little chapel. It is very interesting. Here is a folder and the visiting hours.
- Is there also a bank close by? I need to cash some traveller's checks.
- Yes, there is a bank at the intersection of Rue de la Gare and Rue du Château—but hurry up, the bank closes from noon to 2 P.M. . . . and it is 11:30, hurry up!

17. AT THE BANK

- I would like to change some traveller's checks, please; they are in dollars.
- Good, do you have any identification?
- Some identification? I don't understand.
- A passport.
- Oh, a passport, here it is.
- For how much?
- For 200 dollars. What is the exchange rate today?
- It is 10.04 francs. Sign here, please. Here, that's 2,040 francs, two 500 F bills, five 100 F bills and four 10 F coins.
- Thank you, that's right.
- You are welcome.

18. ON THE TRAIN

- Excuse me, is this seat occupied?
- No, it's not occupied, it's vacant. Sit down. May I put your suitcase up?
- Yes, thank you.
- Do you wish to read the newspaper?
- No, thank you.
- Where are you going, Miss?
- I am going to Bordeaux.
- What a coincidence, I am going to Bordeaux also.
- At what time does the train arrive in Bordeaux?
- It arrives at 6:30 P.M. And why are you going to Bordeaux?
- I am going to see my sister, my brother-in-law and my nephews. And you?
- I am going to Bordeaux on business.
- Ah, yes, and what business are you in?
- Wine business, import-export, Bordeaux wine. And what is your profession, Miss?
- I am a secretary.
- My wife is a secretary also, in Paris. What a coincidence!
- Your wife?
- Yes, my wife, she works in Paris, we live in Paris, we have three children.
- Do you want to have a drink in the dining-car?
- No, thank you, I am not thirsty, and I am not hungry. Excuse me, I am tired. I am sleepy, I am going to sleep.

19. AT THE HOTEL, THE UNLUCKY GUEST

- Good evening, Sir
- Good evening, Madame. Do you have a room for the night, two persons?
- Do you have a reservation?
- No, we don't have a reservation.
- I regret, Sir, the hotel is full.
- FULL!
- Yes, sorry, we don't have any room.
- Can you recommend another hotel?
- Not tonight, all the hotels are full, a convention you understand.
- It's terrible! My wife is ill and we are tired.
- Wait, I am going to phone Chinon. It's 60 kilometers away, does that matter?
- No, it does not matter.
- Hello, good evening. This is l'Hôtel des Châteaux, in Tours. Do you have a room for two? Yes, yes, it's a small room, without a bathroom, yes, yes, third floor? It's all right?
- Yes, it's all right, thank you.
- Yes, it's all right, thank you. (To the guest): What name?
- Gaveau.
- The name is Gaveau. Goodbye!
- Thank you, thank you very much. Let's go, Monique, we have a room.

20. AT THE HOTEL, THE LUCKY GUEST

– Good evening, Madam.
– Good evening, Sir.
– We have a reservation.
– Yes, what name?
– Dupré, René Dupré.
– Certainly, two persons, three nights, room with bathroom and toilet. Your room is ready, come up with me, the elevator is on the left. I'll take your suitcases. Here is room number 29. After you, enter.
– Thank you.
– Here is the bathroom with the shower, the towels. The pillows are in the closet, and here is the key.
– But there are two beds! We prefer one bed.
– Yes, a big bed!
– A room with one bed—you are lucky! Room number 27 is unoccupied and it has a big bed. Follow me, please.
– Here it is, it's all right?
– 400 francs a night.
– Good, thank you.
– At your service, and have a nice stay! For breakfast, you phone tomorrow morning.

21. BREAKFAST IN THE HOTEL

– Hello, Hello!
– Good day, Miss.
– Good day, Sir.
– Two breakfasts, room 27, please.
– Coffee, tea, chocolate?
– One coffee with milk and one tea.
– All right, one "complete" coffee with milk, and one "complete" tea.
– "Complete"? Excuse me, I don't understand. What does "complete" mean?
– "Complete" means that with the coffee or the tea, you also get croissants, bread, butter, and jam.
– And an egg?
– No, sir, no egg.
– And an orange juice?
– An orange juice, with an extra charge.
– Is the breakfast included in the rate of the room?
– No, sir, it is not included, it's 20 francs.
– All right, then, one complete coffee with milk and one complete tea, and two orange juice, with an extra charge!
– Right away, Sir.

22. DEPARTURE FROM THE HOTEL

- I would like the bill, please.
- What name?
- Dupré.
- Yes, room 27, three nights at 400 francs and three breakfasts at 20 francs, for two people. It's 1,320 francs.
- Yes, that's right. Do you take credit cards?
- Certainly, Sir. Visa, American Express, Mastercharge, Eurocard. Are these your bags?
- Yes, they are ours.
- All right, go get the car in the parking lot. I'll help you with the suitcases. I'll be in front of the door.
- Thank you.
- You are welcome.

23. A STOPOVER AT THE COUNTER IN A CAFE

- Coffee with cream, please, and where is the toilet?
- In the basement, at the end of the hall.
- In the basement?
- Yes, downstairs, the stairway is on the left.
- Thank you.

24. AT A SIDEWALK CAFE

- Sir, sir!
- The waiter: What do you wish to drink?
- A beer for me.
- The waiter: A draft?
- Yes, a draft.
- A cola.
- A white wine.
- An apple juice.
- The waiter: Do you want the menu?
- Yes, I am hungry. I would like a "croque-monsieur."
- Same thing for me.
- A ham sandwich.
- Nothing for me.
- The waiter: Right away.

25. AT THE DEPARTMENT STORE

- Good day, Madame.
- Good day, Miss
- You wish to see something?

- Yes, I am looking for some presents.
- And what kind of presents are you looking for?
- I don't know exactly, I am looking for a present for my sister.
- For your sister? A pretty scarf, maybe, some gloves?
- Yes, a scarf, it's a good idea, and I am also looking for a present for my brother.
- For your brother . . . a wallet?
- Yes, a wallet, and for my mother?
- For your mother, wait . . . some toilet water, some perfume, a little box in Limoges porcelain?
- Yes, a little box in Limoges, it's a lovely souvenir. Now I need a present for my father.
- Ah, a tie, a book?
- Yes, a tie, good idea, and for my niece?
- How old is she?
- She is fifteen years old.
- A necklace or some earrings, a bracelet?
- Yes, a bracelet, and for my nephew?
- How old is he?
- He is ten years old.
- A game "Numbers and Letters"—You have a big family!
- Yes, I have a big family and I don't have much money . . .
- But you have some credit cards.
- Yes, Thank God!

26. TWO CAMPERS IN FRONT OF A REAL ESTATE AGENCY

- What a beautiful house!
- Yes, there is a big kitchen, a living room, a dining room, three bedrooms, two bathrooms.
- A garage and a large garden with terrace and a view on the ocean. What luxury!
- Is the rent expensive?
- I don't know, one must look on the billboard.
- All right, I am looking: "For rent, by the month or by the week, beautiful villa on the Mediterranean, big kitchen, three bedrooms, two bathrooms and . . . a swimming pool. Three thousand francs a week.
- Three thousand francs!
- Yes, alas, it's too expensive for our budget, let's camp.
- Let's camp, life is beautiful!

27. AT THE PERFUME SHOP

- Good day, Miss.
- Good day, Madame. What do you wish?
- I would like to buy some perfume.
- Certainly, you have a preference?

- No, show me several brands, please.
- There, we have Air du temps, Bal à Versailles, Ma Griffe, Calèche, Chanel N°5, Chanel N°19, Madame Rochas, Vol de Nuit, Amazone, all the Diors . . . Diorissimo, Diorama . . .
- That's all?
- No, we have also Vent Vert, Gauloise, Eau de Roche, Magie noire . . .
- What a difficult choice! What do you recommend?
- Opium, Madame, it smells very good, it is fashionable.
- I adore Opium, you wish to smell?
- Yes, it smells very good, how much?
- 150 francs, the little bottle for the purse; 300 francs, the large bottle.
- The choice is very difficult, I'll come back.

28. THE HAPPY HOUR

- What do you want for an aperitif? It's my treat.
- A Vermouth Cassis.
- I'll have a Dubonnet with an ice cube.
- A Ricard for me.
- A Martini.

    A few minutes later . . .

- The waiter: There, a Vermouth Cassis for Madame, a Dubonnet for Mademoiselle, a Ricard for you, Sir, and a Martini for you, sir.
- To your health!
- To yours!
- But, it is not a Martini, it's a Vermouth, it's a mistake!
- No, it is not a mistake, John, in France a Martini is a brand of Vermouth!

29. AT THE RESTAURANT, FIXED PRICE

- Good evening.
- Good evening, a table for two.
- Yes, near the window, please.
- Here?
- Yes, that's very good.
- Do you want an aperitif?
- No, thank you, no aperitif, the menu, please.
- Here is the menu, you have two touristic menus, one at 100 francs and one at 150 francs and you also have the gastronomic menu at 200 francs. There is also the a la carte menu. I'll leave you to make your selection.
- Mmmmmmmmm, the touristic menu is advantageous.
- Why?

- Because it includes the hors d'oeuvre, the first course, the main dish, cheese, dessert and the wine is included.
- Yes, it's advantageous.
- What is your choice?
- The touristic menu at 150 francs.
- And for me the gastronomic menu.
- What an appetite you have!
- It's true, but French cooking is so good!

30. AT THE RESTAURANT, A LA CARTE MENU

- Good evening.
- Good evening, Sir, a table for three, please.
- Inside or outside?
- Inside, it is cold tonight.
- Certainly, this way, is it all right?
- Yes, it is very good.
- Here is the menu, will you have an aperitif?
- O.K. I would like a Cinzano.
- Yes, I'll have an Ambassadeur.
- I wish a St. Raphaël.
- What a choice! What do you recommend?
- As an appetizer, the rabbit paté or the asparagus vinaigrette.
- And to start?
- The salmon in puff pastry or the assorted seafood on a skewer.
- All right, the rabbit paté and the salmon.
- For me also.
- I prefer the asparagus vinaigrette and the seafood on a skewer.
- And for the main dish?
- I will have the sweetbreads. Are they garnished?
- Yes, all the dishes are garnished with a julienne of vegetables.
- Not for me. I prefer the grilled lamb chops with herbs of Provence.
- And I, a rib steak with wine sauce.
- How do you want the steak? Rare, medium, well done?
- Medium.
- All right, the sweetbreads, the lamb chops and the rib steak. Do you want a salad?
- No salad.
- No thank you.
- Would you like the cheese or the dessert?
- Cheese, no dessert.
- A dessert, please.
- Cheese and a dessert.
- We have a pineapple sundae, the house custard or the "delight with strawberries".
- The pineapple sundae.
- The delight with strawberries.
- And which wine with all this?
- A bottle of white, a Muscadet, and a bottle of red, a Côtes du Rhône.

- Two bottles, it's too much! A little pitcher of white, maybe, the house wine?
- Good idea.
- Do you want some mineral water also? Plain or carbonated?
- Yes, a large bottle, some plain water.
- Will that be all?
- Yes, that will be all.

   A little later . . .

- What a good dinner!
- Yes, what a good dinner!
- You want some coffee?
- Yes, coffee for me.
- One coffee.
- One decaf, please and the bill.

31. A DIFFICULT CUSTOMER

- Madame, do you want an aperitif? (a before dinner drink)
- No, thank you, no aperitif.
- Do you want an appetizer?
- No, appetizer, I am not very hungry—What is the specialty?
- Seafood, Madame.
- Seafood doesn't agree with me.
- A steak, then?
- No, I don't eat meat, what vegetables do you have?
- Cauliflower au gratin or peas.
- No, thank you, I don't like cauliflower or peas.
- A salad?
- No salad.
- Some cheese, then?
- No cheese.
- Do you want a dessert? Ice cream, pastry, tart, custard?
- No, thank you, I am on a diet.
- Do you want some wine?
- No, I don't drink wine.
- Some water?
- Yes, I am thirsty, I would like a half bottle of mineral water . . . and the bill.
- That's all?
- Yes, that's all, thank you. One moment, close the window, please, I am cold.
- Certainly, Madame.

32. AT THE PHARMACY

- Good day, Madame.
- Good day, Madame.
- I would like some aspirin.

- It's for you?
- Yes, it's for me.
- A large box or a small box?
- A large box but . . . I am not sick.
- And what else?
- Something for the throat.
- Mmmmmm . . . You have a headache and a sore throat?
- Yes, but . . . I am not sick.
- Mmmmmm . . . perhaps it's a cold—you have a temperature?
- I don't know, I am hot.
- Mmmmmm . . . You have a stomach ache?
- Yes, I have a little stomach ache.
- Are you nauseous?
- "Sick to the heart", in the heart?
- No, "sick to the heart", it means "nauseous", it may be the flu.
- Ah, my God, I am sick, what do you recommend?
- Some aspirin for the headache, some lozenges for the sore throat and the cough, and here is some medication for the stomach and stay in bed—It's 80 francs—Rest, Madame, rest in bed and drink some fruit juice.
- I am a foreigner, I would like the name of a doctor, do you have a recommendation?
- Ah yes, Dr. Vaudequin is excellent.
- Do you have his number?
- 258-63-72.
- Write the number please.
- There, Madame, I have written down the number and . . . rest, rest!

33. THE TELEPHONE AND THE DOCTOR

- I am going to call Dr. Vaudequin.
- I'm dialing his number 258-63-72. 2,5,8,6,3,7,2.
- Hello.
- Hello, Miss, I would like to speak to Dr. Vaudequin, please.
- Who is speaking?
- Madame Duchene.
- You are a patient of the doctor?
- No, I am a foreigner and I am passing through.
- One moment, stay on the line.
- Hello, Dr. Vaudequin speaking. What are your symptoms, Madame?
- Ah, good day, Doctor, I am Madame Duchene. I have a headache, I am nauseous, I have a sore throat and I am coughing.
- Mmmmm . . . Do you have a temperature?
- I don't know, but I am hot.
- Take two aspirin, drink lots of fruit juice, stay in bed and call me tomorrow morning if you have the same symptoms—Rest, Madame, rest—Good bye Madame.

34. IN A TAXI

— Taxi!
— Yes, Madame, where do you want to go?
— To Montparnasse please, to the restaurant "La Coupole"—Is it far?
— No, it's twenty minutes away, but there is a lot of traffic.
— Darn! My friends are expecting me at noon and it's already 11:30. Go fast please.
— Ah, customers! It's always the same story, "Go fast. Hurry up". But what a life!

Later . . .

— We are lucky, it is noon and you are not late, you are three minutes early.
— Thank you, thank you! How much is it?
— Forty francs, please.
— Here are forty francs and five francs for you.
— Thank you.

35. CAR RENTAL

— Do you rent cars?
— Yes, of course, what are you looking for?
— A small car—what are your rates?
— We have the week-end rate from Friday evening to Monday morning. Then we have a special rate for eight days (a week) and for fifteen days (two weeks) or for a month. For how many days do you want the car?
— One week.
— Do you want some insurance?
— Of course.
— The price is 500 francs a week for a small car with insurance. Renault, Fiat, Peugeot, Toyota?
— A Renault.
— Get out your passport and your driver's license, I'll be with you right away.
— Thank you.

36. AT THE AIRPORT

— Pardon, Sir. We are looking for a cab to go to Paris.
— Go out through door number 30. The taxis pass by often.
— What is the cost of a taxi for Paris?
— About 100 francs.
— That's expensive! We are students. Is there a train for Paris?
— Yes, take the bus that goes to the station, the stop is in front of the door number 25. There is a bus every fifteen minutes for "La Gare du Nord" in Paris.
— How much is a train ticket?
— 25 francs.
— It's perfect for us, thank you. Let's take the train!

37. AT THE ZOO

- I feel like going to the zoo!
- Wait, I'll look in the guidebook. Yes, the "Zoo de Vincennes" is very famous.
- Where is it?
- It is at Vincennes, there, southeast of Paris.
- I see, and how does one get there?
- The directions are very clear. We are here at Etoile; we take the subway, direction Vincennes, as far as Saint Mandé-Tourelles, it's direct. There, we get off and we take the bus number 86, at the corner of Avenue Charles de Gaulle and Avenue de Paris. The end of the line is in front of the zoo.

  Later on . . .

- It's a beautiful zoo. I love to look at the animals, the tigers, the lions, the panthers, the elephants, the giraffes.
- I prefer the monkeys, they are so funny.
- And the birds, they are magnificent, and I read in the Michelin guide that there are 600 mammals and 700 birds in this park, which is the richest one of France.
- Yes, and I note with pleasure that the setting is natural.
- What freedom for the animals!

38. AT THE STATION

- I would like to reserve a T.G.V. ticket for Lyon.
- For what date?
- September 5th.
- One-way or round-trip?
- Round-trip.
- First class or second class?
- Second class.
- Smoking or non-smoking?
- Non-smoking. What are the hours of departure?
- There is a departure every half hour.
- And how much time does it take to go to Lyon?
- It takes two hours.
- It's fast!
- Yes, T.G.V. means "train at great speed."
- O.K. So, one round-trip Lyon, second class, non-smoking, September 5th, at 10:15 A.M.
- Here are 600 francs.
- I have one more question. Is there a dining-car in the 10:15 train?
- No, but there is a snack bar. Don't forget to validate your ticket.
- "Validate my ticket"? I don't understand. What does that mean?

- To validate means to insert your ticket in the "composteur," the orange-colored machine near the platform to mark the date. Otherwise, your ticket is not valid and you risk a fine.
- Thank you very much.
- You are welcome.

39. AT THE EIFFEL TOWER

- Shall we go up in the Eiffel Tower?
- Of course, we are in Paris to visit all the monuments.
- We have the choice between the first platform, the second platform or the third platform; what do you prefer?
- Let's go to the third one, the view will be sensational.
- O.K. Here is the line to buy the tickets.

At the ticket window:

- Two tickets for the third platform, please.
- The third platform is closed today.
- Darn! Why is the third platform closed?
- Too many people, Sir.
- Then two tickets for the second platform.
- 44 F. Get in the line. The elevator is in the back, on the right.
- What a crowd!
- Listen, people speak every language, it isn't the Eiffel Tower, it is the Tower of Babel!
- Do you have your map to identify Paris?
- Yes, here it is.

On the tower . . .

- What a view! Paris is gigantic!
- How many inhabitants are there?
- Two million.
- Look, the Seine river, the Palace of Chaillot and all the bridges.
- And the excursion boats on the Seine.
- I see the Sacred Heart Church over there, on the hill.
- Look. The cars are so tiny.
- What a show!
- There. The green area is the Bois de Boulogne and there is La Défense, the new Paris, the little Manhattan with its skyscrapers.
- Let's go down to the first platform, we can have something to eat or drink.
- Good idea. Do you know how many steps there are in the staircase of the Eiffel Tower?
- Yes, there are 1652 steps.
- My goodness!

40. AN ENCOUNTER

- Colette!
- Michele, what a surprise!
- And what a day!
- What did you do?
- I went to the department stores.
- Me too, and to what stores did you go?
- To the "Printemps" and to the "Galeries Lafayette".
- I went to the "Samaritaine".
- What did you buy?
- I have bought many things: a dress, a skirt, two blouses and some shoes—and you?
- I have bought a bag, some pantyhose, a nightgown and two records.
- There are many sales right now, the prices are terrific, but what crowds!
- Did you visit the antique show at the Printemps?
- No, I haven't visited the show, but I have seen some furniture, some pictures, and some rugs in the furniture department.
- I went to the basement and I have looked at dishes, cooking pans, and glasses.
- For you?
- No, I am looking for a wedding present.
- Let's go to the tearoom to have a cup of tea.
- With pleasure!

41. ARRIVAL IN PARIS

- Ladies and gentlemen, we are landing in a few minutes at Charles de Gaulle Airport, return to your seats, fasten your seatbelts, and extinguish your cigarettes. Thank you. It is 2:30 P.M. local time and the temperature is 20 degrees centigrade. Captain Denis and his crew thank you and wish you an excellent stay in France.
- This stewardess is really charming!
- Oh yes. Look! The freeway, the houses, the fields, the gardens, the cars.
- And the boats over there on the river!
- Here we are, we are landing.
- Don't forget your newspaper.
- Oh, now I am going to read French newspapers.
- You speak French well.
- I am learning with a new method, "Entre Nous", do you know it?
- No, but I am counting on you!

www.ingramcontent.com/pod-product-compliance
Lightning Source LLC
Chambersburg PA
CBHW060858050426
42453CB00008B/1014